Populations on the RISE

Contents

On the Rise

What could be cuter than a family of rabbits? What if each rabbit in the family soon has its own family? Then the number of rabbits will multiply.

A **population** is the total number of something in one place. Sometimes animals can outgrow their habitat. Then what happens?

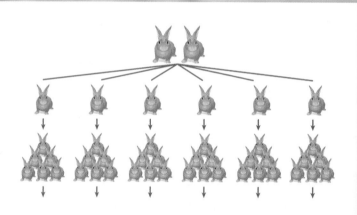

Suppose two adult rabbits have about six baby rabbits. When those six rabbits grow up, they each have six babies. This would be 6 × 6, or 36 rabbits. How many rabbits will be born in the third and fourth **generations**?

Did You Know?

One female rabbit can have up to 8 babies every month.

Lots of Geese

Rabbits are not the only animals whose numbers are rising. During the last 25 years, the number of Canada geese has risen.

When geese fly south, they often find food in farm fields or lawns. They might stop to eat and rest. Some do not go any farther.

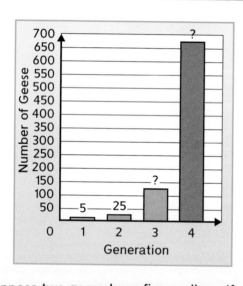

Suppose two geese have five goslings. If these five goslings each have five babies, there will be 5 × 5 or 25 goslings. How many goslings will be born in the third and fourth **generations**?

Pairs of Canada geese
will stay together for life.

These geese do not have **predators**. That allows their numbers to grow. The huge supply of food helps too.

Many geese in one place can cause problems.

Some states along the Atlantic coast have a population of over 100,000 Canada geese.

Canada geese destroy plants that other large birds need to eat. Their droppings **pollute** rivers and streams. They also make parks and playing fields very messy.

As more and more geese arrive, they can create problems in parks. Skip count by 2s to see how their number can grow if 2 geese arrive at a time. Now, what happens if you skip count by 3s? 5s? 10s?

Dealing With Deer

Deer have become more common. New homes are being built where they once lived. Now that the deer live near humans, their numbers are growing. They feast on farmers' crops. They also eat people's gardens.

Populations on the Rise

Deer per square mile
- More than 45
- 30–45
- 15–29
- Less than 15

Central Texas has more than 45 deer per square mile.

Deer do not have to worry about their natural predators. Very few areas are full of wolves and bears. There are many more deer than wolves and bears. The deer population is much bigger.

Deer sometimes eat farmers' crops.

The state of New York is home to about one million deer.

Too many deer can cause problems for drivers. Deer can wander onto the roads and highways. This can cause bad accidents.

Many states are taking steps to keep the number of deer under control.

Deer have caused many car accidents. If 3 accidents are caused each day for one week on a roadway, how many accidents are there in all for the week?

More and More Mosquitoes

Mosquitoes grow in number only in wet areas. Mosquito eggs cannot develop in dry spots. They might lie still for years. They will hatch if there is a lot of rain or still water.

Mosquito eggs need standing water to hatch. Heavier storms have caused the number of mosquitoes to rise quickly.

Mosquitoes might lay eggs in standing water.

Mosquitoes spread disease. This is one reason cities and towns are trying to get rid of this harmful insect.

Populations grow for many reasons. Two main reasons are fewer predators and more food. Changes in how people live and in the weather have also helped change the number of certain animals.

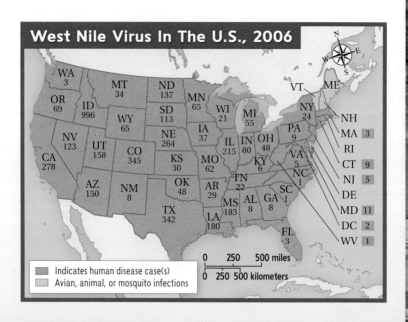

West Nile Virus In The U.S., 2006

WA 3
OR 69
ID 996
MT 34
ND 137
MN 65
WI 21
MI 55
NY 24
VT
ME
NH
WY 65
SD 113
IA 37
PA 9
MA 3
NV 123
UT 158
NE 264
IL 215
IN 80
OH 48
RI
CA 278
CO 345
KS 30
MO 62
KY 6
VA 5
CT 9
AZ 150
NM 8
OK 48
AR 29
TN 22
NC 1
NJ 5
DE
TX 342
MS 183
AL 8
GA 8
SC 1
MD 11
LA 180
DC 2
FL 3
WV 1

0   250   500 miles
0   250 500 kilometers

■ Indicates human disease case(s)
■ Avian, animal, or mosquito infections

TALK ABOUT IT

Mosquitoes have brought West Nile virus to the U.S. Which state had the most human cases in 2006?

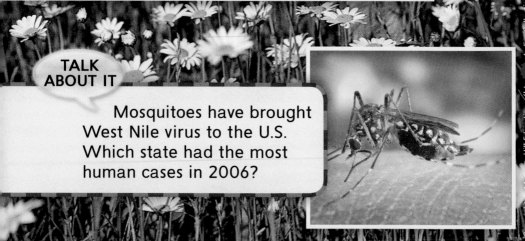

Changes in conditions can make populations rise or fall.

15

Glossary

generations
Entire groups born at the same time. *(page 3)*

predator
An animal that hunts other animals for food.
(page 6)

population
All the members of a single type of organism in
one place. *(page 3)*

pollute
To add harmful substances to air, land, or water.
(page 7)